Let Freedom Ring

The Wilderness Road, 1775

by Laura Purdie Salas

Consultant:
Tom N. Shattuck
Author of *A Cumberland Gap Area Guidebook*
Owner
The Wilderness Road Tours Company
Middlesboro, Kentucky

Bridgestone Books
an imprint of Capstone Press
Mankato, Minnesota

Bridgestone Books are published by Capstone Press
151 Good Counsel Drive, P.O. Box 669, Mankato, Minnesota 56002
http://www.capstone-press.com

Library of Congress Cataloging-in-Publication Data
Salas, Laura Purdie.
    The Wilderness Road, 1775 / by Laura Purdie Salas.
    p. cm.—(Let freedom ring)
    Summary: Discusses colonial America's need for a route to the west, how the Wilderness Road developed, early explorers and settlements along its path, and the impact it had on western expansion.
    Includes bibliographical references (p. 45) and index.
    ISBN 0-7368-1561-9 (hardcover)
    1. Wilderness Road—Juvenile literature. 2. Frontier and pioneer life—Tennessee, East—Juvenile literature. 3. Frontier and pioneer life—Kentucky—Juvenile literature. 4. Frontier and pioneer life—Virginia—Juvenile literature. 5. Boone, Daniel, 1734–1820—Juvenile literature. 6. United States—Territorial expansion—Juvenile literature. [1. Wilderness Road. 2. Frontier and pioneer life. 3. Boone, Daniel, 1734–1820. 4. United States—Territorial expansion.] I. Title. II. Series.
F454 .S25 2003
973.2—dc21   2002008616

Editorial Credits
Carrie Braulick, editor; Kia Adams, series designer; Juliette Peters, book designer; Angi Gahler, illustrator; Kelly Garvin, photo researcher; Karen Risch, product planning editor

Photo Credits
Bell County Historical Society and Museum, 37, 38
Colonial Williamsburg Foundation, cover (inset)
Corbis/Kennan Ward, 8
Hulton Archive by Getty Images, cover, 15
Kentucky Historical Society, 16, 42, 43
National Park Service, 41
N. Carter/North Wind Picture Archives, 10, 19
North Wind Picture Archives, 5, 6, 13, 20, 22, 29, 33, 34
Stapleton Collection/Corbis, 31
Stock Montage, Inc., 27

Table of Contents

Chapter One

Colonists Need Room

Between 1776 and the early 1800s, thousands of settlers gathered their belongings to move west across the Appalachian Mountains. These people faced a journey of more than 200 miles (322 kilometers) on a dangerous stretch of road. The Wilderness Road was muddy, hilly, and rocky. As they traveled, settlers could face attacks by American Indians. But settlers hoped they could start a better life for themselves in the land they called Kentucky.

Around 1775, few permanent settlers lived in Kentucky. By 1800, more than 200,000 settlers lived there. The Kentucky settlers came from different backgrounds. Some had been born in the eastern coastal states. Others were from Ireland, Germany, Denmark, or other European countries. But nearly all of the Kentucky settlers had followed

Thousands of settlers from the eastern United States moved west to Kentucky during the 1800s.

the Wilderness Road. In 1775, a group of men led by Daniel Boone created the path that became the Wilderness Road. This road became one of the most useful and important roads in the history of the United States.

Pushing West

In the early 1700s, British colonists lived along the eastern coast of North America. As people continued to settle in the new territory, the colonies filled up with people. Settlers moved farther west to

Long hunters stayed in Kentucky for months at a time to hunt wildlife.

find land. By the mid-1700s, the western frontier bordered the eastern side of the Appalachian Mountains. These mountains stretched from Canada south beyond the colony of Georgia.

Great Britain's 13 colonies could not support the many settlers who lived there. A great deal of hunting had caused wildlife populations to decrease. Continuous use of the fields caused the soil to wear out and crops to fail. The settlers needed more land.

Many settlers wanted to move west of the Appalachian Mountains. They heard about this land from people who trapped and hunted wildlife for months at a time west of the mountain range. These people were called long hunters. They described huge forests of oak, maple, pine, and walnut trees. They said great numbers of deer roamed the forests, and that large areas of grassland swarmed with buffalo.

Colonists who crossed the Appalachians said the Cherokee Indians called the land Ken-tah-teh. Some people said this word meant "meadowland." Others said it meant "tomorrow," or "the land where we will live." Settlers called the land Kentucky, Kaintucke, or Caintuck.

Barriers to Kentucky

Kentucky sounded like paradise to many colonists in the east. But three main barriers prevented many people from moving there. The French did not want British colonists moving onto land they claimed. American Indians did not want settlers to take over their hunting lands, and no trail existed through the mountains.

The French had claimed North American land west of the Appalachians to the Mississippi River.

The thick forests of the Appalachian Mountains can make travel through them difficult.

The Proclamation of 1763

The British government issued the Proclamation of 1763, ordering colonists not to settle west of the Appalachians. British government officials did not want colonists so far beyond their control. Most colonists ignored the rule.

They wanted to become rich by trapping animals and selling the furs. The French did not want the British to use or take over their land.

Arguments about land ownership also caused many problems between settlers and American Indians. The Cherokee, Shawnee, and other Indian nations had hunted in Kentucky long before French explorers arrived. The Indians thought they would lose their land and hunting grounds if they allowed settlers to move west. American Indians sometimes killed settlers or captured them and kept them as slaves.

In addition to disagreements over land, there was no easy trail to follow over the mountains. Hunters and explorers had to pick their way through the thick forests that blanketed the mountains.

Cumberland Gap

Dr. Thomas Walker was an agent in the Loyal Land Company of Virginia. This company owned the rights to 800,000 acres (323,760 hectares) of land west of the Appalachians. He wanted to sell the land to settlers. But people did not want to buy the land unless they could travel on a path through the mountains to reach it.

On March 6, 1750, Walker left Virginia with five other men to look for a path. Five weeks later, Walker found what he called a "plain Indian road." It was the

Thomas Walker and his group easily passed through the area he called Cave Gap. Later, people began to call it Cumberland Gap.

Warrior's Path. The Cherokee and other Indian nations used the road to travel to hunting and battle areas. It ran from the colony of South Carolina north to New York.

Walker's group traveled up the path. It led to a break in the mountains. This area of land was not covered with thick forests like other mountain terrain. It was easy for the men to pass through. The men passed a large cave near the break, so Walker called the break in the mountains Cave Gap. The path led the men downhill. The men then found a river that they named the Cumberland River.

Into Kentucky

Walker and his men built a small cabin to claim the land. They then headed into Kentucky. They fought their way through groves of tall, tangled brush. Walker climbed a tall tree. He was looking for the rolling, grassy meadows he had heard about. But he never traveled out of the mountains. He wrote in his journal, "As far as my sight could reach, the land was the same as it had been for the past two days. It was time to turn back." Walker was convinced that Kentucky was unfit for settling, and the men returned home.

People had crossed the Cave Gap before. But Walker noted its location so others could place it on maps. After Cave Gap became well known, people started to call it Cumberland Gap instead.

The French and Indian War

In the mid-1700s, both Great Britain and France wanted control of the Ohio Territory. This land lay north of the Ohio River in Pennsylvania and extended north to Canada's border. It includes the present-day states of Ohio, Indiana, and Michigan.

In 1753, the French fought a small battle with colonists from Virginia. The battle led to a war between France and Great Britain called the French and Indian War (1754–1763). Many Indians fought alongside the French. They disliked the British for moving onto Indian land.

In 1763, France and Great Britain signed the Treaty of Paris to end the war. France gave up its claims to Canada and the western territory between the Appalachian Mountains and the Mississippi River. This land included the Ohio Territory.

Closer to the West

By the 1760s, colonists were desperate to settle the west. Immigrants from Europe were pouring into America.

Soldiers from the French and Indian War had been paid with warrants. These pieces of paper could be traded for western land. But American Indians resisted western settlement, and there was still no path through the Appalachian Mountains.

Colonial officials met with American Indian leaders. In 1768, the Iroquois Indians signed an agreement that gave part of their territory to Great Britain. The Cherokee also signed a treaty with Great Britain that gave up part of their rights to Kentucky. The only remaining barrier to western expansion was the Appalachian Mountains.

Great Britain and France fought many fierce battles against each other in the French and Indian War.

Chapter Two

Daniel Boone

Daniel Boone was a woodsman with a love for adventure. He spent a great deal of time exploring and hunting in the wilderness. During the French and Indian War, Boone met an Irish soldier named John Finley. Finley and other soldiers told Boone about Kentucky. Boone was determined to see it for himself.

Growing Up

Born in 1734, Boone grew up at the edge of the wilderness in Pennsylvania. He often explored the woods. Shawnee and Delaware Indians visited his family. They taught Boone a great deal about the wilderness. In 1750, Boone's family moved to North Carolina. There, Boone spent even more time in the woods.

After working as a wagon driver in the French and Indian War, Boone returned to North Carolina and married Rebecca Bryan.

Daniel Boone spent much of his time hunting and exploring in the wilderness.

Hunting in Kentucky

In May 1769, Finley asked Boone to go on a hunting trip. Boone, Finley, and four other men crossed the Appalachian Mountains into Kentucky.

American Indians were a constant concern for the hunters. During the trip, the Shawnee captured Boone and his brother-in-law, John Stewart. The Shawnee took the men's horses, animal hides, and furs. They then let the men go. Stewart later disappeared. Most people believe the Shawnee killed him.

Boone visited Kentucky during a hunting trip in 1769. This painting shows Boone (center) viewing Kentucky for the first time.

During winter, Boone's brother, Squire, and another man arrived with supplies. By spring 1770, Boone and his brother were the only men from the group remaining in Kentucky. The others had returned home. Squire traveled east twice to get more supplies. By spring 1771, the brothers were ready to go home. On the way, a group of Cherokee stole their furs and hides. Boone arrived home penniless after being away from his wife and children for almost two years.

A Family Loss

Boone's visit to Kentucky had been troublesome. But he could not stay away from the wilderness. After visiting Kentucky again, he decided to move his family there. At the time, few people lived in Kentucky.

Boone's family left for Kentucky in September 1773. A small group of settlers traveled with them. One evening, Boone's 16-year-old son, James, and another teenage boy were traveling behind the main group. American Indians attacked and killed the two boys. Saddened by the boys' deaths, Boone and the others turned back toward North Carolina. They would not settle in Kentucky that year.

Chapter Three

Blazing the Wilderness Road

In early 1775, a North Carolina judge named Richard Henderson formed the Transylvania Company. He planned to buy land for the company, sell it to settlers, and create a 14th colony. In March 1775, company officials made a deal with some Cherokee. The company gave the Cherokee money and goods in exchange for a part of Kentucky. Henderson then hired Daniel Boone to create a trail to Kentucky.

A Tiring Journey

Boone quickly gathered about 30 men. The men planned to use axes to hack across 200 miles (322 kilometers) of thick forest. At first, they followed a well-worn wagon road. They then moved onto a narrow trail. Boone rode ahead of the other men to mark trees. The axmen followed Boone's marks and cut down trees to clear the trail.

Daniel Boone and a group of axmen carved the path that became the Wilderness Road through the Appalachian Mountains. This photo shows a part of the road today.

The men faced several challenges. The thick forest was difficult to clear. It was filled with thickets of slender, woody stems called canebrake. The men crossed icy streams and worked in the snow. They climbed steep mountains.

Finally, the group passed through the Cumberland Gap into Kentucky. They turned northwest and followed the Warrior's Path for a distance. The flat trail was a relief for the tired axmen. But the men's labor was not over. After they left the Warrior's Path, they cut through more miles of thick brush.

Boonesborough became one of Kentucky's first settlements. It enclosed about 1 acre (.4 hectare) of land.

In mid-March, the men left the hills. Clover-covered grasslands spread out before them. The open land looked perfect for farming and building.

Trouble with American Indians

Boone's group made a camp. As they slept, gunshots and war cries rang out. The Shawnee attacked the camp, killing two men and stealing some horses. Boone and the axmen quickly built a fort for protection.

By April, Boone's group had reached the Kentucky River. The men built a fort and cabins. This settlement at the river's south bank was later named Boonesborough. The path that Boone and the axmen carved through the mountains was called Boone's Trace. It was renamed the Wilderness Road after it became a popular travel route.

Revolutionary War

In April 1775, the Revolutionary War (1775–1783) began. Colonists fought to gain independence from Great Britain.

British military leaders encouraged American Indians to attack colonists' Kentucky settlements more often. As a result, many settlers returned east by the end of the summer.

The Boone Family Moves

The British and American Indians tried to keep settlers from moving west. But Boone was determined to live in Kentucky. The Boone family moved to Kentucky in the fall of 1775. When they reached Boonesborough, the family became the first permanent settlers of Kentucky. Settlers only considered a settlement permanent if women and children lived there.

Small groups of settlers soon came to Boonesborough. The settlers survived the winter with barely enough food or supplies.

Boone rescued his daughter, Jemima, and her two friends from the Shawnee during the summer of 1776.

What about Henderson's Claim?

At first, Henderson's Transylvania Company operated smoothly. But in spring 1776, Boonesborough's settlers became dissatisfied with the company's practices. Henderson tried to persuade Virginia lawmakers to support his company. These officials did not believe Henderson owned Kentucky land. He had paid for it, but the Cherokee he dealt with did not have the authority to sell him the land. Henderson did not make any money from the land he claimed in Kentucky, and Daniel Boone never got paid for blazing the Wilderness Road. Instead, Virginia claimed Kentucky.

Attacks on Boonesborough

In 1776, conflicts with American Indians continued to be a problem for the settlers of Boonesborough and other nearby settlements. In July, Boone's teenage daughter, Jemima, and two of her friends took a canoe ride on the Kentucky River. Shawnee Indians kidnapped them while the girls floated along the bank. Within a few days, Boone and a group of men surprised the Indians while they were cooking and rescued the girls.

Boonesborough continued to be attacked by Indians throughout the next few years. In February 1778, the Shawnee captured Boone. Boone later escaped. During his time with the Shawnee, Boone learned they were planning a major attack on Boonesborough. Boone helped the settlers prepare for the attack.

In late summer, the Shawnee raided the settlement. The settlers resisted the attack for several days. The Shawnee tried to build an underground tunnel to get underneath the fort's walls. But rainfall caused the tunnel to collapse. The Shawnee then stopped the attack. It had been one of the fiercest and longest battles between settlers and Indians in Kentucky.

Kentucky, the Late 1770s

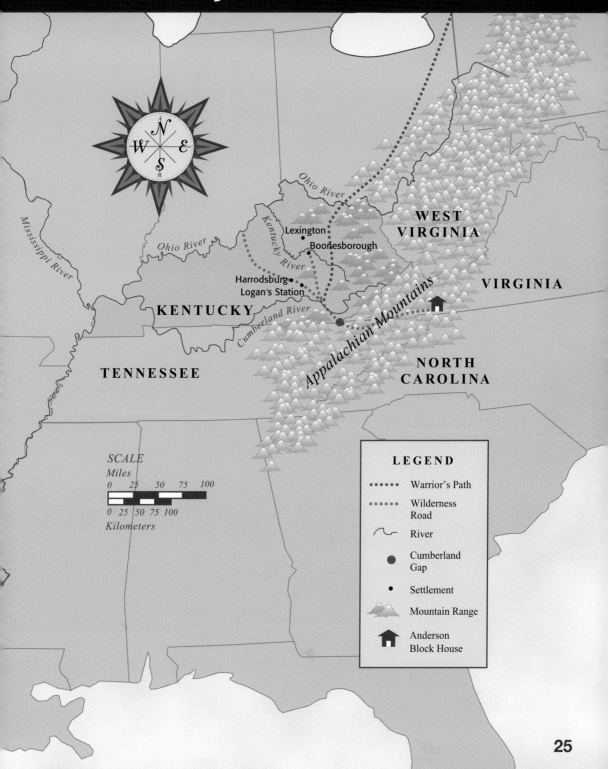

Mississippi River

Ohio River

Ohio River

Kentucky River

Lexington

Boonesborough

WEST VIRGINIA

Harrodsburg

Logan's Station

KENTUCKY

Cumberland River

Appalachian Mountains

VIRGINIA

NORTH CAROLINA

TENNESSEE

SCALE
Miles
0   25   50   75   100

0 25 50 75 100
Kilometers

LEGEND
.... Warrior's Path
.... Wilderness Road
River
Cumberland Gap
• Settlement
Mountain Range
Anderson Block House

Chapter Four

Moving West

Attacks by Indians on Boonesborough and other settlements proved to easterners that western settlement was dangerous. But thousands of settlers were willing to take the risks to reach the land they had heard so much about.

Traveling the Wilderness Road

When a group prepared to travel west, they packed up everything they owned. They put pack saddles on their horses. They then filled the large baskets hanging from the saddles with food, tools, bedding, clothes, and other supplies. Some settlers also filled wagons with supplies.

People who wanted to move west gathered at a building in Virginia called the Anderson Block House. Settlers traveled in large groups for protection from Indians.

Settlers moving to Kentucky sometimes traveled part of the way by horse and wagon.

Settlers could travel by wagon until they got to Cumberland Gap. There, the road narrowed. Settlers left their wagons at Martin's Station on the east side of Cumberland Gap. They then walked or rode horses in single file. A few men rode at the front and end of the line as guards. American Indians in the area often raided travelers on the Wilderness Road and stole their belongings.

Travelers had other problems on the Wilderness Road. At some places, the trail was so steep that the horses had trouble carrying the packs. The settlers then had to carry the packs. Some packs spilled in the road and in streams. Floods and wet bogs made walking difficult. Animals became injured. The conditions caused some travelers to become sick.

After settlers arrived in Kentucky, they needed to make a choice. Settlers had extended the Wilderness Road west soon after Boonesborough was established. This western route led to Logan's Station and Harrodsburg. Travelers also could turn north and follow the Wilderness Road to Boonesborough and Lexington. Most settlers went west because it was an easier route.

Thousands of settlers moved to Kentucky in the late 1770s. In 1779, more than 20,000 settlers moved there.

Early Kentucky Life

Early settlers in Kentucky worked hard. Most settlers built cabins in the woods and then cleared the land nearby to plant crops.

The settlers spent much of their time making sure they had enough to eat. They grew corn, melons, beans, pumpkins, turnips, and squash. They raised cattle, hogs,

American Indians and early Kentucky settlers fought many battles. Indians often attacked settlers' cabins at night.

In the News

Soon after the Wilderness Road was widened, the following article was published in *The Kentucky Gazette* newspaper:

THE WILDERNESS ROAD from Cumberland Gap to the settlements in Kentucky is now compleated. Waggons loaded with a ton weight, may pass with ease, with four good horses. Travellers will find no difficulty in procuring [obtaining] such necessaries as they stand in need of on the road; and the abundant crop now growing in Kentucky, will afford the emigrants a certainty of being supplied with every necessary of life on the most convenient terms.

and sheep. They hunted turkey, buffalo, deer, and other wild game.

As more settlers came to Kentucky, small groups of cabins grew into large settlements. Each one had a store, a school, and a church. People built roads to connect settlements. Farms grew larger. Soon, farmers planted crops and raised animals to sell, not just to feed their families. Settlers began to sell goods and ship livestock to people in the eastern United States. They used the Wilderness Road as the main shipping route.

A Wider Road

In 1792, Kentucky became the 15th state. More than 100,000 people had traveled the Wilderness Road on their way west. Most of them settled in Kentucky. Some people traveled south to the area that later became Tennessee or north to present-day Ohio.

The first governor of Kentucky was Isaac Shelby. In 1795, Shelby decided to widen the Wilderness Road to 30 feet (9 meters). At this width, wagons could travel the entire length of the road. After it was completed in October 1796, the wider road allowed the businesses and people in Kentucky to easily move goods to eastern states.

Isaac Shelby decided to widen the Wilderness Road so wagons could follow the entire length of it.

Chapter Five

The Glory Days End

By the late 1700s, the Wilderness Road needed repair. Potholes covered the road, and wagons would sometimes break after hitting them. Parts of the road were very steep and muddy. Settlers began to look for other routes west.

New Paths West

In 1796, workers built the Pennsylvania Road. This gravel road connected Philadelphia to Pittsburgh. Some westward travelers followed the road to Pittsburgh. They then floated on rafts down the Ohio River to Kentucky.

Another option for travelers was the National Road, also called the Cumberland Road. This crushed stone road was the country's first federal highway. The United States government had paid

By the late 1700s, many settlers used other routes to travel west. Some settlers floated on rafts down the Ohio River to reach Kentucky.

to have it built. The first section of the road was completed in 1818. It connected the Potomac River in Maryland with the Ohio River. Settlers then floated down the Ohio River to Kentucky.

Many settlers traveled on the National Road to Kentucky during the early 1800s. In 1838, the road was extended to reach Springfield, Ohio. In 1841, the road reached Vandalia, Illinois.

The Civil War

Interest in the Wilderness Road and Cumberland Gap grew during the Civil War (1861–1865). Southern states had broken away from the United States to form their own country, the Confederate States of America. The Northern states fought to keep the United States together. Both the North and South considered the Wilderness Road an easy attack route.

In 1861, the South took over the Gap. The next year, the Confederate army abandoned the forts it had built in the area to fight in another location. The Northern army soon took over the Gap and prepared to protect the North from an expected attack. But the attack never came. Instead, the Confederate army went around the Cumberland Gap into Kentucky.

By the war's end, control of the Gap had passed between the North and South four times. Some small fights took place there, but no major battle ever occurred.

Chapter Six

The Wilderness Road Today

Today, much of the Wilderness Road is gone. Over the years, people have cleared the land to construct buildings and plant crops. Other roads and highways lie on top of the Wilderness Road. Many people drive along sections of the Wilderness Road without realizing it.

Parts of the Wilderness Road still exist. Some parks and forests contain sections of the Wilderness Road. Visitors to these areas can walk or bike along the road.

A Smoother Road

In 1907, workers rebuilt a dangerous part of the Wilderness Road called the Devil's Stairway. This 2.5-mile (4-kilometer) stretch of road went through Cumberland Gap and crossed the Cumberland Mountains. This stretch of mountains is part of the western Appalachians,

Today, some highways in the Cumberland Gap area lie on top of the Wilderness Road.

extending from southern West Virginia to northeast Alabama. The Devil's Stairway had many curves and steep hills. Workers blasted away dangerous sections of the road and paved it with crushed limestone.

In 1908, the Ford Motor Company produced the first Model T. Many people bought this affordable car. At the time, the United States had fewer than 700 miles (1,127 kilometers) of paved highways. As one of the paved roads, the Wilderness Road through the Cumberland Gap was a popular travel route.

Today, park workers want to restore the Wilderness Road to its original condition. This photo of the Wilderness Road was taken about 1890, before much of the road's development.

Saving the Road

By 1940, the United States had many highways.
People traveled on the Wilderness Road less
frequently than they had in the past. Government
officials in Virginia, Kentucky, and Tennessee
wanted to preserve the road. They wanted people
to remember how important the road had been for
travelers in the past.

In 1943, federal government officials created
the Cumberland Gap National Historical Park. The
21,000-acre (8,499-hectare) park is located where the
borders of Kentucky, Virginia, and Tennessee meet. It
includes the Cumberland Gap and part of the
Wilderness Road.

Back to the Original

The curving, narrow highway through the
Cumberland Gap was dangerous even after it was
paved. In the early 1990s, people living nearby called
the area "Massacre Mountain." On average, more
people died in car crashes on this section of road
than on many of the country's other highways.

The National Park Service wanted to make car travel on the road safer. In 1996, workers built two tunnels, each 4,600 feet (1,402 meters) long, through the Cumberland Mountains. The tunnels cut through the mountains near Cumberland Gap. Today, cars travel through the tunnels instead of across the mountains.

Park officials plan to restore the Wilderness Road through the Cumberland Gap to its original condition. They want the road to look much like it did between 1780 and 1810. Workers have dug up 2.5 miles (4 kilometers) of the old highway leading through the Gap. They have poured 250,000 cubic feet (7,075 cubic meters) of dirt over the road. They want to recreate the curving, wandering route of the original Wilderness Road. Park workers also plan to plant more than 22,000 trees in the area.

The National Park Service plans to complete the project in 2003. Visitors then will be able to walk along the road and remember the courage of the settlers who trudged along it on their way to Kentucky.

Today, cars safely and easily pass through the Cumberland Gap tunnels.

TIMELINE

Boone begins traveling to Kentucky with his family, but the family returns home after Shawnee Indians kill his son and another teenage boy.

The Revolutionary War ends; thousands of settlers begin traveling to Kentucky.

Thomas Walker becomes the first settler to identify the Cumberland Gap and place the area on maps.

Boone rescues his daughter and two of her friends from the Shawnee.

| 1750 | 1769 | 1773 | 1775 | 1776 | 1783 |

Daniel Boone travels to Kentucky with five other men to hunt.

March: Boone and a group of men blaze the Wilderness Road to Kentucky and establish Boonesborough.

April: The Revolutionary War begins; the British encourage American Indians to attack Kentucky settlers.

The first section of the National Road is completed, connecting the Potomac and Ohio Rivers.

The federal government creates Cumberland Gap National Historical Park in an effort to save part of the Wilderness Road.

Workers widen the Wilderness Road to 30 feet (9 meters) so wagons can travel the length of the road.

The National Park Service builds two tunnels through the Cumberland Mountains.

1796	1818	1907	1943	1996	2000

The National Park Service works to restore the Cumberland Gap and the Wilderness Road in Cumberland Gap National Historical Park.

The federal government paves the Devil's Stairway, a section of the Wilderness Road through the Cumberland Gap.

Glossary

axmen (AKS-men)—men who are skilled at using an ax

bog (BOG)—an area of wet, spongy land

brush (BRUHSH)—a thick growth of shrubs and small trees close to the ground

canebrake (KANE-brayk)—a thicket of plants that have narrow, woody stems

colony (KAHL-uh-nee)—land governed by another country; people who leave their own country to settle in a colony are called colonists.

expansion (ek-SPAN-shuhn)—the process of making a territory larger

immigrant (IM-uh-gruhnt)—a person who comes to another country to settle

long hunter (LONG HUHNT-er)—a woodsman who spent months or years in the wilderness, hunting and trapping animals

raid (RAYD)—a sudden, surprise attack on a place

treaty (TREE-tee)—a formal agreement between two or more groups of people or nations

warrant (WOR-uhnt)—an official piece of paper that gives permission to do something

For Further Reading

Boraas, Tracey. *Daniel Boone: Frontier Scout.* Let Freedom Ring. Mankato, Minn.: Bridgestone Books, 2003.

Green, Carl R. *Blazing the Wilderness Road with Daniel Boone in American History.* In American History. Berkeley Heights, N.J.: Enslow Publishers, 2000.

Stefoff, Rebecca. *First Frontier.* North American Historical Atlases. New York: Benchmark Books, 2001.

Todd, Anne M. *Cherokee: An Independent Nation.* American Indian Nations. Mankato, Minn.: Bridgestone Books, 2003.

Todd, Anne M. *The Revolutionary War.* America Goes to War. Mankato, Minn.: Capstone Press, 2001.

Places of Interest

Cumberland Gap National Historical Park
U.S. Highway 25E South
P.O. Box 1848
Middlesboro, KY 40965-1848
This 21,000-acre (8,499-hectare) park is located where the borders of Virginia, Kentucky, and Tennessee meet. Visitors can learn about the region's history and hike a section of the old Wilderness Road.

Daniel Boone National Forest
1700 Bypass Road
Winchester, KY 40391
The 670,000-acre (271,149-hectare) forest remains much the same as when Boone hunted in the area.

Fort Boonesborough State Park
4375 Boonesborough Road
Richmond, KY 40475-9316
The park is the site of a reconstructed fort that Boone and his men built upon arriving in Kentucky.

Old Fort Harrod State Park
P.O. Box 156
Harrodsburg, KY 40330-0156
Visitors can see a replica of a fort that settlers built here in July 1774.

Thomas Walker State Historic Site
HC 89, Box 1868
Barbourville, KY 40906-9603
Visitors can see a replica of the cabin Thomas Walker built after crossing Cumberland Gap in 1750.

Internet Sites

Do you want to learn more about the Wilderness Road?
Visit the FACT HOUND at *http://www.facthound.com*

FACT HOUND can track down many sites to help you.
All the FACT HOUND sites are hand-selected
by Capstone Press editors. FACT HOUND will fetch the best,
most accurate information to answer your questions.

IT IS EASY! IT IS FUN!
1) Go to *http://www.facthound.com*
2) Type in: 0736815619
3) Click on "FETCH IT" and
   FACT HOUND will put you
   on the trail of several helpful links.

You can also search by subject or book title. So, relax
and let our pal FACT HOUND do the research for you!

Index